D1252529

Classic Cons
and Swindles

CRIME, JUSTICE, AND PUNISHMENT

Classic Cons and Swindles

Josh Wilker

Austin Sarat, GENERAL EDITOR

CHELSEA HOUSE PUBLISHERS
Philadelphia

Chelsea House Publishers

Editorial Director Richard Rennert
Production Manager Pamela Loos
Art Director Sara Davis
Picture Editor Judy Hasday
Senior Production Editor Lisa Chippendale

Staff for CLASSIC CONS AND SWINDLES

Senior Editor John Ziff
Editorial Assistant Kristine Brennan
Designer Takeshi Takahashi
Picture Researcher Gillian Speeth
Cover Illustration Robert Gerson

3 5 7 9 8 6 4 2

Library of Congress Cataloging-in-Publication Data

Wilker, Josh.
Classic cons and swindles / Josh Wilker; Austin Sarat, general editor.

    p. cm. — (Crime, justice, and punishment)
Includes bibliographical references and index.
Summary: Discusses some of the ways swindlers can take an
honest person's money, describing various scams, con
games, and hoaxes that have been perpetrated in the past.

ISBN 0-7910-4251-0 (hardcover)

1. Imposters and imposture—Juvenile literature. 2.
Swindlers and swindling—Juvenile literature. 3. Fraud—
Juvenile literature. [1. Swindlers and swindling. 2. Fraud.]
I. Sarat, Austin. II. Title. III. Series.
HV6691.W55 1997
364.16'3—dc21   96-53205
                                                      CIP
                                                       AC

Contents

CRIME, JUSTICE, AND PUNISHMENT

Fears and Fascinations:

An Introduction to Crime, Justice, and Punishment

By Austin Sarat

We live with crime and images of crime all around us. Crime evokes in most of us a deep aversion, a feeling of profound vulnerability, but it also evokes an equally deep fascination. Today, in major American cities the fear of crime is a major fact of life, some would say a disproportionate response to the realities of crime. Yet the fear of crime is real, palpable in the quickened steps and furtive glances of people walking down darkened streets. At the same time, we eagerly follow crime stories on television and in movies. We watch with a "who done it" curiosity, eager to see the illicit deed done, the investigation undertaken, the miscreant brought to justice and given his just deserts. On the streets the presence of crime is a reminder of our own vulnerability and the precariousness of our taken-for-granted rights and freedoms. On television and in the movies the crime story gives us a chance to probe our own darker motives, to ask "Is there a criminal within?" as well as to feel the collective satisfaction of seeing justice done.

Fear and fascination, these two poles of our engagement with crime, are, of course, only part of the story. Crime is, after all, a major social and legal problem, not just an issue of our individual psychology. Politicians today use our fear of, and fascination with, crime for political advantage. How we respond to crime, as well as to the political uses of the crime issue, tells us a lot about who we are as a people as well as what we value and what we tolerate. Is our response compassionate or severe? Do we seek to understand or to punish, to enact an angry vengeance or to rehabilitate and welcome the criminal back into our midst? The CRIME, JUSTICE, AND PUNISHMENT series is designed to explore these themes, to ask why we are fearful and fascinated, to probe the meanings and motivations of crimes and criminals and of our responses to them, and, finally, to ask what we can learn about ourselves and the society in which we live by examining our responses to crime.

Crime is always a challenge to the prevailing normative order and a test of the values and commitments of law-abiding people. It is sometimes a Raskolnikov-like act of defiance, an assertion of the unwillingness of some to live according to the rules of conduct laid out by organized society. In this sense, crime marks the limits of the law and reminds us of law's all-too-regular failures. Yet sometimes there is more desperation than defiance in criminal acts; sometimes they signal a deep pathology or need in the criminal. To confront crime is thus also to come face-to-face with the reality of social difference, of class privilege and extreme deprivation, of race and racism, of children neglected, abandoned, or abused whose response is to enact on others what they have experienced themselves. And occasionally crime, or what is labeled a criminal act, represents a call for justice, an appeal to a higher moral order against the inadequacies of existing law.

Figuring out the meaning of crime and the motivations of criminals and whether crime arises from defiance, desperation, or the appeal for justice is never an easy task. The motivations and meanings of crime are as varied as are the persons who engage in criminal conduct. They are as mysterious as any of the mysteries of the human soul. Yet the desire to know the secrets of crime and the criminal is a strong one, for in that knowledge may lie one step on the road to protection, if not an assurance of one's own personal safety. Nonetheless, as strong as that desire may be, there is no available technology that can allow us to know the whys of crime with much confidence, let alone a scientific certainty. We can, however, capture something about crime by studying the defiance, desperation, and quest for justice that may be associated with it. Books in the CRIME, JUSTICE, AND PUNISHMENT series will take up that challenge. They tell stories of crime and criminals, some famous, most not, some glamorous and exciting, most mundane and commonplace.

This series will, in addition, take a sober look at American criminal justice, at the procedures through which we investigate crimes and identify criminals, at the institutions in which innocence or guilt is determined. In these procedures and institutions we confront the thrill of the chase as well as the challenge of protecting the rights of those who defy our laws. It is through the efficiency and dedication of law enforcement that we might capture the criminal; it is in the rare instances of their corruption or brutality that we feel perhaps our deepest betrayal. Police, prosecutors, defense lawyers, judges, and jurors administer criminal justice and in their daily actions give substance to the guarantees of the Bill of Rights. What is an adversarial system of justice? How does it work? Why do we have it? Books in the CRIME, JUSTICE, AND PUNISHMENT series will examine the thrill of the chase as we seek to capture the criminal. They will also reveal the drama and majesty of the criminal trial as well as the day-to-day reality of a criminal justice system in which trials are the exception and negotiated pleas of guilty are the rule.

When the trial is over or the plea has been entered, when we have separated the innocent from the guilty, the moment of punishment has arrived. The injunction to punish the guilty, to respond to pain inflicted by inflicting pain, is as old as civilization itself. "An eye for an eye and a tooth for a tooth" is a biblical reminder that punishment must measure pain for pain. But our response to the criminal must be better than and different from the crime itself. The biblical admonition, along with the constitutional prohibition of "cruel and unusual punishment," signals that we seek to punish justly and to be just not only in the determination of who can and should be punished, but in how we punish as well. But neither reminder tells us what to do with the wrongdoer. Do we rape the rapist, or burn the home of the arsonist? Surely justice and decency say no. But, if not, then how can and should we punish? In a world in which punishment is neither identical to the crime nor an automatic response to it, choices must be made and we must make them. Books in the CRIME, JUSTICE, AND PUNISHMENT series will examine those choices and the practices, and politics, of punishment. How do we punish and why do we punish as we do? What can we learn about the rationality and appropriateness of today's responses to crime by examining our past and its responses? What works? Is there, and can there be, a just measure of pain?

CRIME, JUSTICE, AND PUNISHMENT brings together books on some of the great themes of human social life. The books in this series capture our fear and fascination with crime and examine our responses to it. They remind us of the deadly seriousness of these subjects. They bring together themes in law, literature, and popular culture to challenge us to think again, to think anew, about subjects that go to the heart of who we are and how we can and will live together.

*   *   *   *   *

We often think of crime as violent and the criminal as an anonymous stranger victimizing the unsuspecting. *Classic Cons and Swindles* tells the story of another kind of crime, one in which guile, not force, is the key method of operation, and trust, not fear, defines the relationship of criminal and victim. From rigged card games to complex investment schemes, from imposters to swindlers, from 19th-century pastimes to scams perpetrated with and through state-of-the-art technology, this book provides a lively catalog of crimes in which persons are victimized, in part, as a result of their own greed, their own desire to make an easy dollar. To study cons and swindles is to study the ingenious ways in which some seek to profit by playing on the weaknesses of others. It is to study the sometimes ambiguous line between honest, though inflated, claims and outright misrepresentations. This book describes a criminal world populated by devious rogues who are sometimes storied for their ability to take us in, but who nonetheless do real damage and render us all more vulnerable and less trusting. *Classic Cons and Swindles* reminds us of the great diversity of criminal activity and of the way it is woven, almost seamlessly, into the fabric of our daily lives.

A Custom-Made Trap

A group of well-dressed professionals, businessmen of a particular sort, arrive in a new city with a job to do. One of these men checks into a hotel under an assumed name. In the hotel room he unpacks from his sleek briefcase a checkered gaming cloth with numbers and stars and metal caps on it. He also unpacks a deck of playing cards. With nothing to do but wait, this man bides his time by practicing card tricks. He can do anything he wants to with the cards. His hands are hummingbird quick. He can pull the ace of spades out of thin air a thousand times in a row.

While this man waits, the second member of the partnership roams the city. His job is to find someone who has money and who might be persuaded, one way

A city street teeming with people of all ages and backgrounds, each a potential mark for con artists working time-tested scams such as bunco.

or another, to part with it. He wanders through bars and convention halls and hotel lobbies and city squares, blending in wherever he goes, until he finds what he's looking for. He travels widely. The possibility exists that he, or someone like him, will train his experienced, discerning eyes, at one time or another, on you.

Maybe he is watching as you inadvertently show a large roll of traveler's checks while paying for a souvenir. Maybe you happen to be dressed in expensive clothes. Maybe he sees in your eyes a certain innocent gleam, the unguarded look of someone who has never been swindled. He watches you and sees a chance to make some money.

The second part of his job begins. He is to learn all he can about the person he has targeted. If the man is good at what he does, you will have no idea that you are being interviewed. Like all the people who make a living in his line of work, this man, a stranger to you, will be able to quickly and deftly intuit what kind of person you are comfortable talking to and he will become that person. He'll be a starry-eyed professor of philosophy. He'll be a loud, slightly tipsy off-duty cop. He'll be a decent, honest, soft-spoken family man. He'll be whoever it is necessary for him to be. You'll get lost in the conversation, and emerging naturally from the pleasant talk will be information about your past history, about places you have lived in or visited, about your friends and relatives, about your likes and dislikes. You'll be oblivious to the fact that you are giving out strands of information that the man and his professional colleagues will weave into a tight net, a custom-made trap.

The day after your seemingly harmless conversation, a second stranger will approach you. He is the third member of the professional partnership. As the man coaxing aces out of thin air continues to bide his time in the hotel room and as the man with the keen eyesight moves on to ferret out more money, the third man comes toward you, smiling broadly. He says your

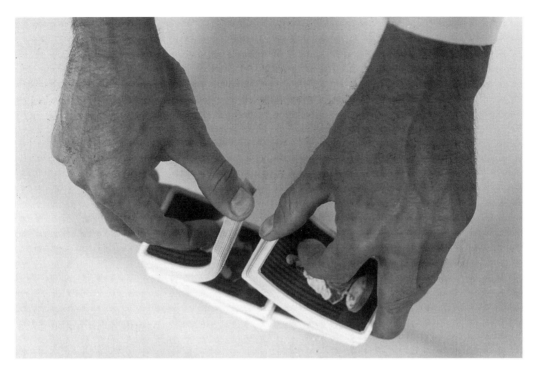

name. He says, "Don't you remember me?"

At first you don't. He's a stranger. But he begins telling you things about your own life that no stranger would know. He might say he is a distant cousin, naming the relatives that connect the two of you together, or he might say he is a long-lost friend, naming the school the two of you went to. He uses the information his partner garnered to chip away at any skepticism you might have about his supposed identity.

Meanwhile, a fourth man arrives at the hotel room. He and the man with the deck of cards begin to prepare for your imminent arrival. They go about their business like two experienced butchers calmly sharpening their knives.

Their partner is also going about his business, which happens to be making you feel lucky. He'll make you feel lucky that the two of you chanced to meet and, moreover, just plain lucky to be alive. This man's specialty is making the sky a little bluer, the air a little

There is no way to win at bunco because the dealer is a magician with cards. He can produce whatever card he wants without arousing the slightest suspicion that he is cheating.

sweeter. He can turn an average day into a day of celebration and can wheel a day of celebration toward a night of joyous, uninhibited revelry. Deep into the night you'll still feel strong and young and lucky. You'll feel luckier than ever. That's when the man posing as your friend mentions that he knows a place where the two of you can go to take advantage of your overbrimming good luck.

When you get to the nondescript hotel room, you find that the game your friend has told you about, a game called bunco, is already in progress. One man is shuffling and dealing cards to another man, and the numbers on the cards are then added up to see if they correspond to a winning number on the checkered sheet spread over the table. The game looks simple enough, and you and your friend join in.

There are countless variations of bunco. Some versions are played with dice, others with cards. In all of the variations the money seems at first to flow toward the player as if from a powerful geyser. You and your friend win big and keep on winning. The third player leaves eventually; he was there only to make the game appear legitimate. The gushing river of money has blinded you by now to any possible questions of legitimacy. The game of bunco began the day before when a stranger looked at you and saw money, and the game accelerates toward its conclusion as you see money and go blind.

The dealer, the man who can make the ace of spades appear at will, senses when this blindness has set in and at that point makes sure that the cards in your hand add up to a number corresponding with one of the metal caps on the bunco sheet. This, he tells you, is "the conditional." For you to continue playing and to have a shot at a $10,000 grand prize, you need to put up an amount of money double the amount you have won so far. Your friend, who has also been hit with the conditional, comes up with the money on the spot. He looks to you, as does the dealer.

"Easy money," says your friend, smiling.

"Now or never," says the dealer.

You're not thinking clearly. You are not even your normal self. You are someone 10 times luckier than your normal self. You are the luckiest person in the world. You are seconds away from a $10,000 jackpot. You can close your eyes and see the money. You can take a deep breath and smell it. You can taste it.

"Now or never," repeats the dealer, and you gouge every last cent from your pockets and lay it on the table by the bunco sheet. The next thing the dealer will say is, "You lose."

"IF YOU CAN
BEAT HIM,
YOU DO IT"

I n 1906 the legendary magician Harry Houdini penned a book on cons and scams entitled *The Right Way to Do Wrong*. He spoke, among other things, of the bunco swindle, noting that the word *bunco*, because of the widespread effectiveness of the scam, had come to take on added meaning. Houdini wrote, "Today the word is used to denote almost any swindle where the victim is made to believe he is to receive a large sum of money or valuables and then gets nothing at all."

The bunco scam is just one among many con games and swindles that promise heaven and earth and deliver nothing at all. The number of these scams is impossible to tally—it seems at even a quick glance to

The Charlatan, *by Dutch painter Hieronymus Bosch (ca. 1456–ca. 1516). Though the props have changed, human nature has remained constant, and con artists have never encountered a shortage of gullible victims.*

Magician and escape artist Harry Houdini, who took a keen interest in debunking mind readers, mediums, and other charlatans, also exposed cons and swindles of a more mundane variety.

practically verge on infinity. Con artists like the man with the sleek briefcase who could deal aces from nowhere skirt around the globe as plentiful as shadows. Some of them work alone, using short nickel-and-dime cons to thicken their wallets; others ply their trade within astoundingly intricate webs of illusion, entire teams of swindlers working together over a period of weeks or months or even years to wrest gleaming fortunes away from their victims.

There are cons at work on city streets, in stores, in bars, on carnival midways. There are cons at work in suburban neighborhoods, on skid row, and in the most elite summits of high society. There are cons designed especially to take advantage of the elderly and the sick. There are cons designed to take advantage of people who want all the riches the world has to offer, and there are cons designed to financially cripple those people who want something of a more spiritual nature—an angel's outreached hand, the touch of heaven.

With such a wide variety of ways for a flimflamming bamboozler to divorce his victims from their paychecks, it is difficult to make any sort of blanket statement about all cons and swindles. But in virtually all con games, large and small, the victim will be looked upon with cold, calculating eyes by the swindler. The victim is a sucker, nothing more. The swindler's opinion of the sucker ranges from cool disregard to outright contempt. "You can't make money every day in hustling," remarked a professional grifter, or con artist, named C. R. D. Sharper (a pseudonym) in a book on card and dice scams called *Road Hustler*, "so when the good days come around, you better forget about feeling sorry for [the victims], and just put your head down and make the money." No one escaped the leveling gaze of Sharper and his partners: "Priests, we beat priests, oh yeah, they're good, they dig in their pocket and blow their money as gracefully as anyone else. . . . [E]ven a cripple, if you can beat him, you do it."

If the coldheartedness of a swindler is the engine at the center of many cons and swindles, the awakened greed of the victim is often the gasoline. The bunco scam, for example, depends on the player developing an overpowering thirst for $10,000. A famous 19th-century con artist named George Devol saw that the lust for money often played the starring role in his profession. He wrote in his autobiography, "The sucker feels like he is going to steal the money from a blind

The Mississippi riverboat was the workplace of 19th-century con artist George Devol, who made a fortune from his mastery of the three-card monte scam.

man, but he does not care. . . . It is a good lesson for a dishonest man to be caught by some trick," Devol added, "and I always did like to teach it."

Devol's specialty was a card game called three-card monte, which he played to great profit on Mississippi riverboats and in railroad club cars. The game has moved from boats and trains to city streets, where it thrives today, feeding on the same kind of blinding greed that made George Devol a rich man. Darwin Ortiz, discussing the modern street-corner three-card monte game in a book called *Gambling Scams*, concludes, "When a mark [a potential victim] thinks he smells easy money, his critical faculties evaporate."

In three-card monte, as in the bunco scam, a team of con artists work as a unit to give the impression that the game is both legitimate and potentially profitable to the mark. The leader of the team is the dealer, who shuffles three cards around atop a stack of empty cardboard boxes. The dealer first shows the three cards faceup and then invites all observers to identify, after he has shuffled the cards around facedown, which card is the red queen. Swindlers known as shills pose as players, some winning to make it appear that winning is possible, others losing to give the mark a feeling, during his initial observations of the game, of superiority. There is no way to win at the game, for the dealer is a magician with the cards. He is able to switch one card for another without the switch being detected.

If the potential mark refrains at first from laying money down (perhaps he has heard the not-so-well-kept secret that three-card monte games are crooked), the con artists perform a charade to help coax the cash from his pocket. The dealer will pretend to be momentarily distracted just before starting to shuffle the cards, looking away from the cards as a shill reaches forward

Three-card monte as played at the turn of the century on a Coney Island beach. Today the game flourishes on city streets everywhere.

and bends the corner of the red queen. The dealer appears not to notice the stunt, and after the cards are shuffled, the bend in the one card remains. The mark now sees that he can't possibly lose and bets on the bent card. The dealer has, however, deftly smoothed the bend in the red queen while shuffling and has put an identical crease in another card.

Three-card monte, which uses the flash and dash of the fast-talking dealer to attract the attention of potential suckers, is the most visible of the myriad short cons that infest city streets all over the world. Three-card monte games can be seen from a block away. Most other street cons tend toward invisibility. A victim won't know what he or she is involved in until it's much too late.

The con known as the pigeon drop is a street scam that sneaks up on its victims. But it does share with the three-card monte scam a dependence on the greed of the victim. The more popular version of this con game begins when con artist A strikes up a conversation on the street with the potential victim. As the two walk and talk, a pocketbook is spotted on the street, preferably by the victim, but if the victim is oblivious con artist A will point it out. A third person arrives on the scene as con artist A and the victim are inspecting the pocketbook to find a substantial sum of money inside. This third person is also a con artist. Con artist B will demand a piece of the action, a demand calculated to awaken in the mark demands of his or her own. More often than not the mark will think, "Why shouldn't I get part of the money too?"

Con artist B will demand that everyone involved show "good-faith" money. This good-faith money is to be offered up, con artist B will explain, to show that each member of the threesome is a person with means, and not, for example, a street criminal with nothing who might take advantage of the other two. The two con artists are able to show their money quickly. The

For hundreds of years, beggars have been a part of the urban landscape. While many are indeed down on their luck, some are merely working a simple and profitable con.

mark will follow suit, sometimes even taking a trip to the bank to match the hefty good-faith sums displayed by the con artists. One of the con artists will then employ sleight of hand to replace the mark's money—which the con artist seems to wrap in a handkerchief along with a third of the found money—with shreds of cut-up newspaper.

A variation of the pigeon drop takes into consideration that not all people will be blinded by greed. If con artist A intuits that the potential victim is not going to jump at the chance for some easy money, a different kind of pigeon drop will ensue. The con artist will pose as a person in distress, someone from a small, faraway town who is lost and daunted by the big city. The mark will be ensnared in the con not by greed, but by a desire to help. After involving the mark further, perhaps by getting him or her to help find an address that in actuality doesn't exist, the con artist will ask if the mark could hold his money for a while. "I'm just too afraid to walk around this city with so much cash," he says. The trust the con artist puts in the mark usually boomerangs from the mark back to the con artist. "Let me bundle up my money with yours," the con artist will say. The mark trusts the con artist, watching as the money is seemingly bundled up in a handkerchief. This con comes to the same conclusion as the previous swindle, with the grifter out of sight and confetti from a handkerchief raining down on the sidewalk.

Another crooked nickel-and-dime street hustle that feasts on something other than a victim's greed is the begging scam. A man known as Blind Charlie, who wasn't blind at all, stood outside Macy's every day for years with a sign that read, "I AM BLIND. PLEASE HELP ME." He raked in enough change during his career to buy four apartment houses. Another fraud named Charlie, Breadline Charlie, made a handsome living by scattering bread on the sidewalk, waiting for a well-dressed person to happen by, then pouncing on the bread like a starving animal, devouring it, and turning a pathetic gaze (and a couple of upturned, empty palms) toward the well-dressed pedestrian.

The two Charlies presumably came up with their scams on their own. If they were just starting out in the fraudulent-begging business now, they might not have to be so self-reliant. Recently an institution named Fagin Prep (named for the character in Charles Dickens's *Oliver Twist* who tutors children in street crime) opened its doors in New York City to teach people effective begging scams, such as posing as a respectably attired businessman who has just had his wallet stolen and needs to "borrow" cab fare home (he'll mail you a check when he gets there), or, a Fagin Prep favorite, faking a medical emergency (as an instructional guide for the school points out, "they don't want you to die at their feet").

WHERE THERE'S A WALLET, THERE'S A WAY

Three-card monte, the pigeon drop, and begging scams are some of the short cons (cons that chug along effectively with a minimum of time, crooked manpower, and misleading details) that inhabit city streets. City streets offer anonymity and a large pool of potential victims, two things that grifters working the short con look for in a workplace. But swindlers don't confine their turf to such locales. They go wherever the money is. Where there's a wallet, there's a way to get inside it.

And where there's an automated teller machine, there's a way to get inside many wallets. One way swindlers have devised to use bank machines to their advantage is to screw shut the slot where the customer's money is supposed to come out. The customer makes a withdrawal, finds that the money does not come out, and leaves the machine to find help. The swindler comes out of hiding with a screwdriver and finishes the

From the swank cocktail lounge to the neighborhood taproom, bars provide a fertile field for con artists. The victims include patrons and bartenders alike.

29

transaction. In another ATM con a grifter dresses in a security guard's uniform and, telling approaching customers that the machine is out of order, explains that he has been stationed thusly by the bank in order to personally take their deposits. The swindler cannot make any money on those people looking to make withdrawals, and he probably won't find every potential depositor gullible enough to hand over their money to him. But the swindle has worked in the past, its effectiveness resting largely on the grifter's acting ability and the victim's lack of caution. This scam pales in comparison to the biggest of all ATM swindles, in which an entirely phony ATM is wheeled into a busy area, such as a shopping mall. The machine looks real and acts real. Needless to say, the machine gives out no money, instead only taking in deposits and the secret password numbers of each cardholder. The next day, the machine is gone.

To a grifter working the short con, the next best thing to a cash machine is a cash register. Short cons that prey on shop merchants, cashiers, and bartenders abound. The simplest type of con that hovers around a cash register is the change snafu. In the most popular money-changing ploy a grifter seeks out a crowded store that has a young, inexperienced cashier. He makes a small purchase with a big bill and then begins asking for his change in smaller denominations than what the cashier is giving him. While keeping up a constant patter to distract the cashier, the grifter continues to change his mind about the bills he wants, asking first for two tens and a twenty, then for six fives and a ten, then for just two twenties, and so on, until the cashier has little idea how much money she has already handed over the counter. The grifter, using sleight of hand to pocket bills as the confusion mounts, usually walks out of the store with twice as much money as he walked in with.

Another one-person con is the Christmas card envelope switch. The swindler buys a Christmas card

Banking by automated teller machine seems safe and reliable, yet con artists and swindlers have found ways to make ATM technology work for them.

and asks the cashier for a $20 bill to put in the card. The grifter hands the cashier a pile of crumpled bills, which the cashier counts and finds to be a dollar short of 20. Apologizing profusely, the trickster gathers up the crumpled bills and gives the card—which the cashier saw, or thought he saw, a $20 bill go into—as collateral. Then he leaves, promising to return with the extra dollar. He doesn't return and there is, of course, no money in the card.

Bars, like stores, have cash registers. They also have, as an added enticement for the short-con grifter, patrons whose mental faculties have been considerably muddied by the intake of alcohol. A drunk mark is an easy mark. One old grifter is said to have bamboozled boozers by pretending to be thoroughly soused himself and bellowing repeatedly, "I'll bet anyone in the house I can bite my own eye!" He would keep at it until one of the patrons took him up on the seemingly impossible bet simply to shut him up. With the money on the bar top, the old man would pluck out his glass eye and bite it. He'd then go on to challenge the sucker to a double-or-nothing bet on whether or not he could bite his other eye. The stooge, his reason now impaired not only by drink but also by anger, would again slap his money down, sure that the old man couldn't have two glass eyes. At this point the grifter would pluck out his false teeth and with them chomp his good eye.

While this preposterous-proposition bet may be nothing more than a legend, countless short cons do go down in the dim light of the saloon. One that Carl Sifakis, author of *Hoaxes and Scams: A Compendium of Deceptions, Ruses, and Swindles*, estimates is worth between $25,000 and $50,000 a year for the solitary grifter begins much like the glass-eye con above. The grifter pretends to be knee-crawling drunk, so hammered he barely knows where he is. He throws a lot of money around throughout the night and eventually asks the bartender, or even another patron, to cash a legitimate-looking payroll check. This request will often inspire in at least one person the greedy impulse to shortchange a drunk. Whoever steps forward and cashes the check has invariably been blinded by his or her own greed to the possibility that the check could be fraudulent. Which, of course, it is.

The "put and take" swindle, which involves two con artists working together, is another bar con that preys on the greed of the victim. The first swindler, known as the inside man, engages a bartender in a friendly conversation. After chatting for a while he pulls out a many-sided top with numbers on it. Each number has either the letter *p* or the letter *t* preceding it. The two men engage in a betting game with the top: Each time the *p* comes up the spinner "puts," or gives money to the other man, and each time the *t* comes up he "takes." The inside man eventually confides to the bartender that the top is "gaffed," or fixed to offer predictable results. When spun clockwise, it will always come up "take"; when spun counterclockwise, it will always come up "put." The grifter says he really doesn't have much use for the device, but he hazards a guess that the bartender has the perfect job for using it. The bartender sees a chance to augment his salary by fleecing drunk patrons at the rigged betting game and buys the top from the grifter.

After allowing enough time, at least a couple of days, for the bartender to grow supremely confident in

A crowded store at the peak of the holiday shopping season provides ideal conditions for various money-changing cons performed at the expense of inexperienced cashiers.

A potential—albeit unwitting—participant in the pedigreed dog swindle, a profitable two-person scam that victimizes bartenders anxious to make a quick buck.

his new money-maker, the second grifter, known as the outside man, enters the bar. The bartender naturally sees the stranger as a potential sucker in his betting game and so pulls out his gaffed top. The outside man, however, uses quick, magician-like hands to switch the bartender's top with an identical top that works exactly opposite to the first one. The bartender will usually drop a bundle of money to the outside man, sure that his top, which has worked so well for him up to this point, will again start doing what it's supposed to do.

Over the years, the most popular inside man–outside man con has been something called the pedigreed dog swindle. In this con the inside man enters a bar with a dog and, offering $10, convinces the bartender to watch the dog for a few minutes. The outside man enters after the first grifter has left and begins gushing about what a fine purebred specimen the dog is. He offers the bartender a hefty sum for the dog, usually in the neighborhood of $500. The bartender says he can't sell the dog at this time but tells the buyer to come back later. The outside man leaves, usually upping his bid on the dog by a hundred bucks as he walks out the door. The inside man returns, his shoulders shrunken in dejection. He tells the bartender that his business deal has gone sour. The bartender offers to help him out by buying the dog, often for at least half of what the outside man was willing to pay. The bartender sees a chance to make a quick and easy profit. When the outside man does not return, the bartender will eventually realize he has spent $300 on a mutt.

DARKENING
THE MAGIC

The dimly lit bar is not the only environment that has proven especially conducive to swindling. The carnival midway, with its games and rides, its flashing lights and cotton candy, often seems to work magic on people, ushering them away from the less colorful workaday world. Grifters have learned how to darken this magic, fleecing starry-eyed carnival goers with a host of crooked carnival games.

The game called razzle begins with a feature that is common to many other classic cons and swindles, large and small. The mark steps up to the counter and is enclosed on both sides by high wooden walls. This isolation is something used in different ways by con artists everywhere to keep the mark from making contact with the world outside his or her skewed illusion. Such con-

The carnival grounds, a place of simple, wholesome fun, sometimes has a darker side.

tact—a friend raising questions about the legitimacy of the game, for example—can bring a con crashing down.

The isolated player at razzle will be given a free first turn by the dealer. The dealer throws marbles across a board with numbered holes. The numbers the marbles fall into are added up and that total may or may not correspond to points to be awarded to the player. On that first free turn the player will "get lucky" with a whopping 5 points and be told that he is well on his way to 20 points. The dealer, making a sweeping gesture toward the snazzy merchandise—television sets, microwave ovens, stereo equipment—festooning the wall behind him, will inform the mark that when he wins 20 points he will have his pick of the prizes. This showing of valuable items to the mark is, of course, another feature that razzle shares with countless other cons and swindles. A hunger is awakened in the mark. The free turn is over, so the mark begins digging into his own pocket to play.

The money flows from the mark at a rapidly increasing rate. The dealer continually ups the ante by proclaiming that certain numbers from the marbles correspond to doubling and tripling mechanisms on the points board. The mark begins paying out double and triple the amount he started paying on every turn for a chance at double and triple the booty. The dealer strings the mark along with many psychological ploys, placating him with encouraging words and worthless token prizes. The most effective psychological ploy is the ever-increasing point total: as it inches closer to 20, the mark feels closer and closer to victory and, moreover, sees that if he were to quit before getting there he would forfeit all the money he has already thrown into the game. Carnival grifters say that at this point the mark is "in the chair." The mark is desperate, completely irrational, completely fleeceable, and the grifters comply. They take him for everything in his

pockets, and sometimes the game doesn't even end there. Sometimes the mark begs the dealer to let the game continue just long enough for him to run home and get more money.

One way to tell a crooked carnival game from a straight one is to keep an eye out for any game that has a "points toward 20" component. That's a good clue that the game is polluted. Another clue is in the operator's behavior. Carnivals always have a slew of throwing games—knock over the milk bottles, toss a ball through a hoop, land a softball in a basket, and so on. It's possible to tell whether or not a certain throwing game is run by a flattie (a carnival grifter) by watching how the operator acts. In dirty throwing games the operator will attempt to string the mark along by telling him he hates his boss and wants to see the mark win the game so his boss will lose money. The operator proceeds

Step right up! A carnival hawker may run a legitimate game in which you have a fair chance to win, but then again he may be a flattie—a carnival grifter expert at separating the unwary from their money.

What appears to be a simple game of chance may be rigged. Consider the "Jumbo Cage," shown here. The operator turns the handle to swing the cage and thus roll the dice. The players bet on the total. The catch? An electromagnet placed in a metal money drawer under the table controls the specially made dice.

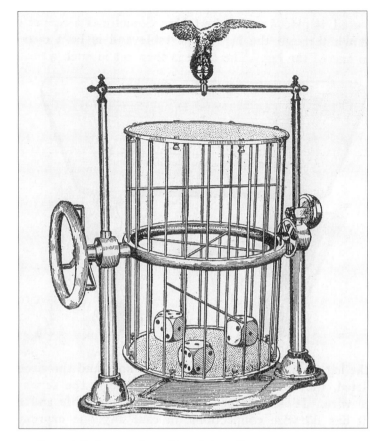

to "coach" the mark, telling him after every unsuccessful throw that he almost had it. The mark, believing that the operator really wants to help him, will keep thinking that his winning throw is just around the corner. But, as cons and swindles expert Darwin Ortiz points out, "If the average person had any idea of the total contempt flatties have for anyone who isn't 'with it' (in the carnival business) they would realize how foolish it is to believe that a game operator really wants to coach you to help you win."

This contempt for the mark, as has been shown already, is something shared by grifters everywhere. They carry it with them through city streets and in stores and bars. And some of them even carry it right up to the front door. Con artists do make house calls.

The Better Business Bureau has estimated that the swindling of homeowners costs Americans upwards of a billion dollars a year. Almost all of these scams are quick jobs, short cons in which the criminals are in and out of the house before the homeowners can figure out what hit them.

The catalog con is the simplest of the house-call cons. It requires only one persuasive con man working alone. He comes to the door with a catalog from a well-known national company. After flashing a phony I.D. card that proclaims his connection to the company, he begins showing off pictures in the catalog of everything from clothing to expensive appliances, then offers what he calls a "10 and 10" deal. The bogus salesman says he can, as a representative of the national company, get the mark 10 percent off the price of any item in the catalog if the mark pays 10 percent of the asking price of the item on the spot. The mark will never get closer to an item he puts money down on than looking at a glossy picture of it.

A more involved and potentially more lucrative con on homeowners begins with two grifters posing as contractors on their way home from a job. They pull into the driveway of the mark and explain that they have materials left over from the job they have just completed. The jacklegs pose variously as painters, driveway resurfacers, or roofers. Rather than taking the extra materials back to their boss—whom, the grifters are quick to point out (as a way of making the con seem more legitimate), they despise—they are willing to sell their materials and services to the homeowner for a greatly reduced price. The homeowner sees it as a chance to get a great deal, almost as though he is getting something for nothing. What he gets is nothing for something. The materials are useless. For example, the "sealant" slapped on the driveway is recycled motor oil.

Another swindle worked at the expense of homeowners is the inspector con. One or two grifters will

Grifters do make house calls. In one popular scam, two con men posing as home inspectors find a problem and mention to the homeowner that they know a reliable contractor who can fix it fast and cheaply. The man in the picture above demonstrates how a supposedly faulty gas line might get "fixed": the grifter merely makes noise in the basement for a few minutes before collecting his fee.

come to the house, posing as inspectors. As in the above scam, the exact nature of this imposture varies. They might say they are inspecting gas lines or electrical lines or water heaters. They might be inspecting for termites or for signs of disease in the trees in the yard. The two common denominators in all the inspector scams are first, that the grifters will look the part, dressing in plausible uniforms and carrying plausible inspector I.D. cards; and second, that whatever dangers they are inspecting the house for they will find.

The inspectors tell the homeowners that they know someone who will be able to offer goods and services quickly and cheaply. If it is the gas line that was "inspected" by the grifters, a third con man, "the gas line expert," arrives to descend to the basement and bang a wrench against some pipes for a few minutes before collecting his pay. If the problem revealed by the grifters was a faulty water heater, a new water heater is installed, which isn't new at all, and in fact in most cases is greatly inferior to the unit it replaced.

A house-call con known as "The Sofa Game" utilizes not two, but three larcenous employees. Two grifters dressed in uniform coveralls lug a sofa to the front door of a house they have cased to make sure that no one is home but the maid. The maid is told that the man of the house, whom they refer to by name, has been chosen by a lodge he is a member of as the recipient of a priceless antique couch for his outstanding community-service work. The maid has heard nothing of this but sees no harm in accepting the gift.

The men in coveralls bring the couch into the living room and drive away. The maid leaves the living room to resume her duties in other parts of the house. The third member of the nefarious team then makes his appearance. Climbing from a secret chamber inside the sofa is a small child. Moving quickly, he gathers as many valuables as he can find and stuffs them and himself back inside the couch. The men in coveralls return, telling the maid that a huge mistake has been made, that the couch is really supposed to go to a family with the same last name on the other side of town. Apologizing for the inconvenience—and moving quickly—the men lug the loot-weighted couch out of the house and drive away again, this time for good.

IMPOSTORS

The next DiMaggio or Mantle? Nope. It's sports impostor Barry Bremen, who showed up for a Yankees-Tigers baseball game in a homemade uniform and proceeded to warm up and sing the national anthem with his adopted teammates before anyone noticed. Bremen also successfully impersonated a baseball player at the 1980 All-Star Game, a 1979 NBA All-Star, and even a Dallas Cowboys cheerleader.

"Some men has plenty money and no brains, and some men has plenty brains and no money. Surely men with plenty money and no brains were made for men with plenty brains and no money." These words, taken from the journal of a man named Charles Orton, could serve as the rallying cry for con artists and swindlers everywhere. Orton wrote them at a time when he was gearing himself up to go from a mere thieving scoundrel (he was wanted in Australia for stealing a horse) to a foul-souled swindler of the highest degree. The scheme, which would, as it steadily unraveled, gain worldwide notoriety for its fat, slovenly originator, was first dreamed up in the same journal pages that contained the swindler's rallying cry. In his brutish hand, Orton scribbled, "Rodger Tichbourne, some day, I hope."

Orton had decided to pose as a man named Rodger Tichbourne. He was, of course, not the first con artist ever to pose as someone he wasn't. In fact, every con

This page: Cassie Chadwick, who convinced America's banking establishment that she was the illegitimate daughter of Andrew Carnegie, one of the world's richest men. Facing page: A forged 1904 note guaranteeing that Carnegie would pay Chadwick $250,000. She used the note to secure part of the $20 million in loans she received.

game, to a greater or lesser extent, depends upon the grifter's ability to create a fraudulent identity. If the con artist can't act his part, the con game, whether it's the bunco scam or the pedigreed dog swindle or a crooked carnival game, will topple like a house of cards. In most con games the swindler is required only to play what would be referred to on stage as a bit part. Charles Orton belonged to a special breed of con artists, those who rested the success of their monumental swindles solely on their mastery of a complex role. Charles Orton was an impostor.

While hiding from the law in Australia under the alias Thomas Castro, Orton had learned that a rich

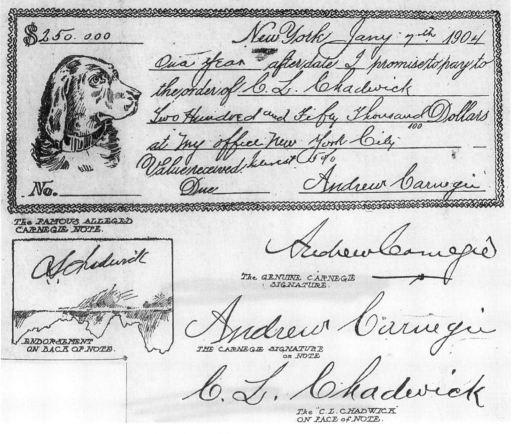

THE $250,000 CARNEGIE NOTE AND ITS SIGNATURE AND ADMITTED HANDWRITING OF MILLIONAIRE.

British aristocrat named Lady Tichbourne was sparing no expense in an effort to find her son, Rodger. The luckless Lady Tichbourne, who had already lost her husband and all of her other children to untimely death, wasn't willing to accept the commonly held belief that Rodger had perished in a shipwreck off the coast of Chile in 1856. Orton, hearing of Lady Tichbourne's search 12 years after the shipwreck, saw a chance to get his hands on "plenty money."

Whether Orton had "plenty brains" was questionable. He didn't seem to consider the fact that he looked nothing like Rodger Tichbourne. Any objective observer could see that Orton was shorter, fatter, and

Kaiser Wilhelm II, on whose supposed authority Wilhelm Voigt arrested the mayor and treasurer of the German town of Kopenick and then made off with the town's funds. The kaiser was so amused by the imposture that he pardoned Voigt.

considerably older than Rodger would have been had he survived the shipwreck. Where Rodger had possessed the most refined manners and a quick and agile wit, Orton could not (and didn't seem to even want to) cover up the fact that he was a thick-voiced, uncultured, addle-brained slob.

What Orton had was chutzpah. Where another, more timid con artist would have balked, the nervy Orton brusquely shouldered forward, in effect stomping straight up to Lady Tichbourne's front door and announcing, "Hi, Mom. I'm home." Besides his hefty gall, Orton also had working in his favor the fact that Lady Tichbourne's discriminating eye had been clouded over by sorrow. Like many con artists before and after him, Charles Orton benefited from the emotional instability of his mark. Lady Tichbourne believed, because she needed to believe, that her long-lost son had returned. Orton's stint as a rich aristocrat might have lasted for the rest of his life had it not been revealed that he lacked a tattoo that the real Rodger had borne on his arm.

A few years after Orton's imposture, an American woman named Cassie Chadwick devised a scheme that would come to rival the Englishman's ruse in notoriety. Chadwick didn't impersonate someone who already existed but instead made up an entirely new person. The act began one day when she was riding in a carriage with a well-connected New York lawyer. She told the carriage driver to make a detour to the house of one of the richest men of the day, industrialist Andrew Carnegie.

Chadwick, who had no connection to Andrew Carnegie whatsoever, exhibited a chutzpah equal to Charles Orton's and marched up to the front door of the Carnegie mansion. While the astonished lawyer watched, Chadwick talked her way in the door by telling the maid that she was looking for a recommendation on a certain housekeeper. Chadwick simply wanted to linger inside the mansion long enough to impress the lawyer. And so, when the housekeeper Chadwick mentioned turned out not to work at the Carnegie mansion, Chadwick simply used her con artist's gift of gab to prolong the conversation with the maid.

After a half hour had passed, Chadwick exited the mansion. In the carriage she "accidentally" let slip from her purse a forged document saying that she had the right to draw on an account in Carnegie's name worth a quarter million dollars. Chadwick then launched into a bogus confession, telling the lawyer she was Andrew Carnegie's illegitimate daughter. "But don't tell anyone," she added.

As the news of her secret identity spread like wildfire, Chadwick researched her new role like the most obsessive of actors. "I had to know every detail about Carnegie's life," she said. The work payed off as seemingly every bank vault from New York to Cleveland swung open for her. Anything with the Carnegie name attached to it worked like a master key in the financial world. She passed $7 million in forged securities onto one ecstatic banker in Cleveland and all told took out upwards of $20 million in loans. Chadwick was undone only when her checkered past, which had included stints as a prostitute, a begging-scam artist, and a forger, caught up with her.

A German shoemaker named Wilhelm Voigt had a checkered past of his own. By the time he got the idea, in 1906, for a scheme that would soon gain him a reputation as one of the most audacious impostors of all time, he had served a total of 27 years in prison for a variety of petty crimes. The plan took shape slowly. First he got his hands on a used military uniform, the garb of a captain in the Prussian army. He began, privately, to practice barking out orders like a military leader, and he took to strolling around town in his uniform to get used to it. The scrawny cobbler noticed that

Not every impostor is looking for monetary gain or notoriety, as Ferdinand Waldo Demara, Jr. (above), proved. Demara's many roles included deputy sheriff, college professor, prison counselor, monk, zoologist, and surgeon. Not bad for a high school dropout.

people seemed to give him more respect when he wore the uniform.

When he felt that he had the role of a Prussian army captain down, he marched to a section of Berlin where soldiers were hanging around and without pause ordered 10 of them to follow him on a mission. The soldiers fell in line behind the impostor, and Voigt led them to a small town outside Berlin called Kopenick. "At the command of His Majesty the Kaiser," Voigt exclaimed to the mayor of the town, "you will be taken to Berlin as my prisoner." The mayor was arrested and sent back to Berlin under the armed guard of some of the soldiers Voigt had commandeered. Kopenick's town treasurer, whom Voigt also arrested, was to follow, escorted by the remaining soldiers. Voigt himself requisitioned the town funds, walked to the nearest train station, changed into his regular clothes, and went home.

The fraudulent Prussian captain was soon collared by genuine officers of the law. He spent just a short time in jail, however, gaining a pardon from a highly amused Kaiser Wilhelm. The "Captain of Kopenick" became something of a celebrity, and one rich Berlin woman even supplied him with a generous retirement pension, calling him a "National treasure."

An impostor who stands out from all others by virtue of the wide variety of roles he mastered was a man named Ferdinand Waldo Demara, Jr. Throughout his life the high school dropout posed convincingly as, among other things, a biologist who did cancer research, a zoologist, a deputy sheriff, a soldier, a Trappist monk, a prison counselor, a hospital orderly, and a college professor with a Ph.D. in psychology.

Demara was an expert forger. The documents he created opened doors for him, and once he was in the door his astounding acting skills kept his various impostures rolling along. The fact that he was also, by most accounts, a genius undoubtedly aided his various deceptions. This was never more evident than when Demara posed as a lieutenant surgeon in the Canadian navy during the Korean War. Though he had never been to medical school, Demara was able to successfully perform major operations during the harshest of battle conditions. He was so good—some claimed he never lost a patient—that his imposture was eventually jeopardized. An organization wishing to pay tribute to his surgical wizardry uncovered the startling truth that their man was an utter fraud.

Demara's story shows that on some level the con artist isn't always concerned just with money. There is something else that draws a person to a life of illusion and deception. Con artists take the reality that most people accept unquestioningly and turn it upside down. It would be simpler to understand the motives of a swindler if the tampering with reality were done solely for financial gain. But that is not always the case. A con artist may also be drawn to his shady profession by a desire to appear to others as something he is not—a person of consequence, a rich, important, powerful person. He may be drawn by a desire to use lies to manipulate and control. Or he may be drawn by the sheer thrill of the crime, the heart-pounding feeling that comes from knowing that with one false move the whole invented world will crumble. Ferdinand Demara was drawn to his life of illusion by the thrill of turning the world upside down. When asked why he had lived the life of a deceiver, he replied, "Rascality. Pure rascality."

The Perfect Victims

One morning in the early 1800s Guiseppe Balsamo awoke and decided that he was not the broken-down hustler he seemed to be. He was not a man who had spent his life as a forger, a swindler, a liar, a lousy magician, a teller of inaccurate fortunes, a pimp, a cheater, a thief, a counterfeiter, and an all-around bad seed. He was not even, he decided, Guiseppe Balsamo anymore. He was Count Alessandro Di Cagliastro, a man of undeniably noble stature who just happened to be 1,800 years old.

The con artist formerly known as Balsamo devised his new persona as a way to help hawk an elixir he called "The Wine of Egypt." He claimed that the cureall medicine had bestowed upon him his astonishing longevity and promised that it could fix any health problem, large or small. Amazingly, Di Cagliastro was not laughed out of town. People wanting and even needing to believe that the cure to what ailed them was in the count's magic potion soon made the impostor a

For those whose "mental ignition" was a bit sluggish, Joseph "Mighty Atom" Greenstein offered a spark—herbs. Greenstein was one in a long line of quacks peddling cures for all of life's physical, mental, and spiritual maladies.

Guiseppe Balsamo, aka Count Alessandro Di Cagliastro, a spry 1,800-year-old. The secret to his longevity? An elixir, called "The Wine of Egypt," that he kindly sold to the sick in the early 19th century.

rich man. The lifelong swindler had finally found the perfect victims. The elixir sold so well that Di Cagliastro began offering 40-day health retreats that featured daily doses of the useless medicine intermixed with fasts, hackneyed philosophical speeches, and the joyless ingesting of roots.

Di Cagliastro was one in a continual line of swindlers who prey upon the sick. Those who have a way with deception are rarely as harmless as the rascally impostor Ferdinand Demara. Di Cagliastro, like others in his often-sinister profession, utilized the desperation of a sick person as his partner in crime. Con artists zero in on human weakness. Often, perhaps to salve their consciences, they view their marks as greedy liars, no better than themselves. The victim of a con game may indeed have as his or her weakness a desire to get something for nothing. But often victims are looking for more than just money. They may be lonely and are looking for a friend. They may feel their lives lack purpose or excitement or meaning or romance and so drift into a swindler's trap looking for something to fill the voids. Or, like the people Di Cagliastro made his money on, they may just feel bad, physically ill, and they want to feel better.

The selling of bogus elixirs is a con game that continues to this day. Among the latest reported cases is that of Dr. Qi, an Asian-American woman who raked in money from pills, sold for $160 per bottle, that she claimed could cure hepatitis and liver cancer. A 1996 *New York Daily News* exposé revealed not only that "Dr." Qi was not licensed to practice medicine anywhere in the world but also that the pills she sold were nothing more than aspirin.

A crook of the lowest kind named Norman Baker chanced to go a little beyond the scope of Dr. Qi's scam. Instead of simply selling expensive pills, Baker set up what he advertised as a cancer treatment center. After collecting exorbitant entry fees from them, he fed his stricken customers ineffectual flavored water. Baker was eventually brought to trial for malpractice, but not until he had made upwards of $4 million on the fleecing of terminally ill patients. He got off easy—a four-year jail sentence and a meager $4,000 fine—because most of his victims had died before being able to take the witness stand.

Senior citizens serve as another favorite target of con artists whose specialty is preying on the weak. These swindlers will zero in on one or more of the afflictions plaguing the elderly: failing health, financial insecurity, feelings of disconnection from the world around them, feelings of loneliness, feelings of isolation. It is this last problem that serves the con artist best. As seen in the crooked carnival game called raz-

Before the courts put him out of business, Norman Baker (shown here) collected more than $4 million from desperate cancer patients. He treated them with flavored water.

zle, in which high walls are set up on either side of the mark to restrict his vision to the con game, the isolation of the mark is of paramount importance for the success of many swindles—and the elderly are particularly vulnerable. Often senior citizens get cut off from their families and friends and so have no one around who might cast a revealing light on the dark workings of a con game.

In one prototypical elderly con, two grifters set their sights on an old woman who has recently lost her husband. One of the swindlers, himself an older man, gradually befriends the woman. As with the con artists in the bunco scam, this grifter is able to intuit what kind of person the old woman is comfortable with and to become that person. He gains her trust by showing her a policeman's badge and saying that he is a plain-clothes officer protecting elderly people from con artists. He gains her sympathy by confiding that he too has lost his spouse recently. This is a ploy to cement their friendship and to isolate the two of them from the rest of the world. "Most people don't know what you and I have to go through," the swindler will tell his mark.

He then disappears for a few days, enough time for the old woman to realize that she has come to depend on his company. He returns to tell her that he has been investigating a criminal plot to swindle some elderly people in the neighborhood, including her. If the grifter has done his job well, the woman's dependence on him will increase. He will be more than just her friend. He will be, in an increasingly confusing and harsh world, her protector.

He says he is going to catch the criminals, but he needs her help. The second grifter makes his appearance, posing as a high-ranking official at the old woman's bank. The second man tells the old woman that they can catch the criminals if she withdraws all her funds from her savings account and takes the

money to an office, supposedly connected to the bank, across the street. Then, he explains, when the criminals go to draw on the account, it will come up empty and they will be caught red-handed. The older grifter stands nearby, offering encouragement. The con ends, as so many do, with an empty bank account and a quick disappearing act on the part of the grifters.

Essential for the above elderly con to work through to its stinging conclusion is the grifters' ability to manipulate and profit from the complex emotions, such as loneliness and grief and fear, of the old woman. Another complex human emotion that con artists have been able to exploit throughout the ages is the desire for some kind of connection with a spirit world, a hunger for another, higher reality that explains, gives meaning to, and eases the pain of this world. "The mortal yearning for Paradise is very strong indeed," wrote

Growing old in our society often means loneliness, isolation, and bewilderment at the rapid changes characteristic of modern life. These feelings make the elderly prime targets for con men and swindlers who specialize in preying on the weak.

Richard De Mille in a book debunking a spiritual huckster named Carlos Castaneda, "and anyone who promises to lead us there is trusted."

A woman named Maxine Asher gained the trust of her marks by promising to take them to the paradisiacal city of Atlantis. Though the underwater metropolis is generally believed to exist only in myth, Asher sheared a score of suckers at Pepperdine University for $2,800 apiece to go a-searching for Atlantis off the coast of Spain. All they found was water.

A century and a half or so earlier, around the time

Count Alessandro Di Cagliastro was pawning himself off as an 1,800-year-old, a tavern owner named Mary Batemen reported that her hen had begun to lay eggs on which were inscribed the promise, "Christ is coming." She said God had told her in a dream that her hen would lay 14 eggs, and after the 14th would come Armageddon. She made her money from the growing crowds at the tavern by telling them that, come Armageddon, they could gain admittance into heaven by possessing pieces of paper with Christ's initials on them, which she happened to be selling for one shilling apiece. Armageddon was postponed by a skeptical doctor who, when snooping around the tavern, happened upon Mary Batemen as she was shoving the 14th egg (marked by her own hand with corrosive ink) up the business end of her tired and ill-humored hen.

A WORLD OF LIES

The swindle that would shuck Tony and Nick Fortunato for $100,000 began when a man handed them a business card reading, "T. Remington Grenfell, Vice President, Grand Central Holding Corporation." The business card was but the first of a blizzard of bogus details. By the time the long con was over, the brothers, Italian-American immigrants who ran a thriving fruit dealership, would be stumbling around as if snow-blind.

The man who said his name was Grenfell told the brothers that the corporation he worked for wanted to sell the information booth at New York City's bustling Grand Central Station. People making too many unnecessary queries were clogging up the main floor at the station. Ticket sellers, Grenfell told the brothers,

Since its completion in 1883, the Brooklyn Bridge has been "bought" by a host of shrewd investors. A con artist named George C. Parker made selling the span his bread and butter.

61

would take over the responsibility of giving out information, and the booth would be rented out to merchants.

The con man told them that the rent would be $2,000 a week and that to secure the booth they would have to pay the first year's rent in advance. The Fortunatos said they needed time to think about it, to which Grenfell replied that if they were not interested the company would be willing to rent to the fruit dealers who happened to be the Fortunatos' prime competitors. The long con got longer as the vice president brought the marks to an office suite in a building adjacent to Grand Central Station. Grenfell and his partners had outfitted the place to look unmistakably like a busy office, complete with receptionists and phones ringing off the hook. The vice president took the Fortunatos to the office occupied by the president of the company.

The president played the part of a busy man with no time for such trifling affairs as the one the Fortunatos were involved in. The vice president had to intervene on their behalf to keep the brusque executive from rescinding the offer of renting out the information booth. The brothers, attracted to the deal by the possibility of such a "Central" location and pressured into making a snap decision by the deft manipulations of the con men, scrounged up the $100,000 and delivered it to the con men later that day.

The following day the Fortunatos showed up at Grand Central Station with a gang of carpenters. A fracas between the carpenters and bewildered information-booth workers ensued. The Fortunatos led legitimate Grand Central Station officials to the office suite and found it completely empty. Apparently the bitterness of the brothers Fortunato never abated. For the rest of their lives they made weekly visits to Grand Central Station to hurl obscenities in the general direction of its information booth.

Like Grenfell and his partners, a swindler named

Barry Minkow had a taste for the big scores that come with the long con. By the time he was 16 years old, Minkow knew how to gain the confidence of people with money. "I was absolutely sure that I was in good hands," said one of his many victims after the teenage swindler's lie-fueled empire of the mid-1980s had collapsed.

New York City's Grand Central Station. In the foreground is the information booth for which fruit sellers Tony and Nick Fortunato paid $100,000.

In 1920 Charles Ponzi (shown here) pioneered an investment swindle that is still around today.

He seemed born with the con artist's skill to change his identity like a chameleon whenever it suited his needs. "No one ever knew the real Barry," said a high school classmate. "He had different personalities around different people."

Minkow also possessed that most important of qualities for the true grifter: a total lack of conscience. He had no qualms about lying routinely to friends and family and at one point even stole a $2,000 string of pearls from his grandmother. With all his qualifications, he could have worked any con game on earth. He could have succeeded at the put and take or bunco or the pigeon drop or any other of the countless short cons infesting the world. But he didn't. He went for the big money.

Barry Minkow became a millionaire by the time he was 18 years old by working an investment swindle called a Ponzi scheme. The con game, named after its first known practitioner, an Italian-American banker named Charles Ponzi, is simple. The first round of investors in a (fraudulent) business venture are paid off at a great profit by the money from a second round of investors. This great profit serves as a clamorous advertisement for the business venture. Potential investors see the money the first round of investors are making and want a piece of the action. Charles Ponzi's version of the scheme worked so well that the rush of people wanting to give him money almost created a riot. According to a *New York Evening World* report from the summer of 1920:

> The passion for investment with the new Italian banker swept over Boston until it took half of Boston's police force to subdue the enthusiasm of a throng of prospective investors that overflowed the banking office, through the corridors, down the stairs, and into the street, blocking traffic.

Barry Minkow's own Ponzi scheme began with the baby-faced grifter convincing people to invest in his

carpet-cleaning company. The swindle snowballed, as all effective Ponzi schemes do, when word got out that the carpet-cleaning business (which, in actuality, was no more than a hollow prop) was making money hand over fist. Minkow helped things along by hiring a public relations expert so he could use television and newspapers to his advantage. It worked like a charm, and soon an abundance of stories in print and on TV spotlighted the fine, upstanding young entrepreneur and his booming business. Minkow received a commendation from the mayor of Los Angeles and began appearing in antidrug television commercials (though he was secretly using steroids, artificially beefing up his own appearance as the Ponzi scheme beefed up the appearance of his company). Minkow, at an age when he wouldn't even be allowed to buy a beer in most states, was able to turn the media into a major partner in his con game.

Silver-tongued former swindler Barry Minkow addresses a group of bankers on how to avoid fraud. As a teenager, Minkow made at least a million dollars from his own Ponzi scheme—and in the process conned the news media and the mayor of Los Angeles.

Where some see a celebrated Paris landmark, others see . . . well, a whole lot of scrap metal. Count Victor Lustig made his living selling the Eiffel Tower for scrap to the City of Light's less culturally discriminating.

Unlike the grifters in the Grand Central Station con, Minkow didn't get away clean. The number of disgruntled investors grew so large—as inevitably happens in all Ponzi schemes—that Minkow finally had to answer their many questions in a court of law. Minkow's phony business was revealed, and the teenage millionaire was unceremoniously tossed in jail.

There is often a price to pay for living a life of deception. Minkow wasn't the only con artist to get caught. Charles Ponzi himself came to know his way around a jail cell. George C. Parker, whose specialty was selling the Brooklyn Bridge, died under lock and key at Sing Sing. Count Victor Lustig, the renowned hawker of the Eiffel Tower to scrap-metal dealers, also drew his last breath in jail, as did, among other lesser-known bamboozlers, the impostor Cassie Chadwick and the 1,800-year-old elixir salesman Count Alessandro Di Cagliastro.

C. R. D. Sharper, the card and dice hustler, recognized that danger is part of the routine in a world of lies, listing the ability to run swiftly as an utter necessity in his line of work. "I know it sounds silly, but I have run out of many parties where I thanked my lucky stars that at least I could run a mile." Sharper punctuated his comment by recalling a time when one of his partners couldn't get away: "[T]hey beat [him] almost to a pulp, and he was an older man."

Perhaps the worst danger in the life of a grifter is that one who blurs the lines between truth and fiction, between right and wrong, may at some point get lost in the fog. The impostor Charles Orton, after spending most of his life in jail, died a penniless madman who had come to believe totally that he actually was the aristocrat Rodger Tichbourne. Another swindler, named Oric Bovar, who conned his marks into believing he was the second coming of Jesus Christ, also veered fully into madness, ultimately offering to prove he was who he said he was by walking out his high-rise window. He believed he would be able to float.

Further Reading

Akst, Daniel. *Wonder Boy*. New York: Charles Scribner's Sons, 1990.

Allen, Bud, and Diana Bosta. *Games Criminals Play*. Susanville, Calif.: Rae John Publishers, 1981.

Anderson, Harry. *Games You Can't Lose*. New York: Pocket Books, 1989.

Greene, Robert W. *The Sting Man: Inside Abscam*. New York: E. P. Dutton, 1981.

Henderson, M. Allen. *Money for Nothing: Rip-offs, Cons and Swindles*. Boulder, Colo.: Paladin Press, 1986.

Houdini, Harry. *The Right Way to Do Wrong*. Boston: Harry Houdini, 1906.

Jay, Ricky. *Learned Pigs & Fireproof Women*. New York: Warner Books, 1986.

Lindskoog, Kathryn. *Fakes, Frauds, and Other Malarkey*. Grand Rapids, Mich.: Zondervan Publishing House, 1993.

Maxa, Rudy. *Dare to Be Great*. New York: William Morrow & Co., Inc., 1977.

Nash, Jay Robert. *Hustlers and Con Men: An Anecdotal History of the Confidence Man and His Games*. New York: M. Evans & Co., 1976.

Ortiz, Darwin. *Gambling Scams*. New York: Dodd, Mead & Co., 1984.

Prus, Robert C., and C. R. D. Sharper. *Road Hustler*. Lexington, Mass.: Lexington Books, 1977.

Sante, Luc. *Lowlife*. New York: Farrar, Straus & Giroux, 1991.

Sifakis, Carl. *Encyclopedia of American Crime*. New York: Facts on File, 1982.

———. *Hoaxes and Scams: A Compendium of Deceptions, Ruses, and Swindles*. New York: Facts on File, 1993.

Wade, Carlson. *Great Hoaxes and Famous Imposters*. Middle Village, N.Y.: Jonathan David Publishers, 1976.

Glossary

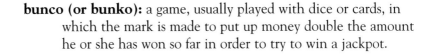

bunco (or bunko): a game, usually played with dice or cards, in which the mark is made to put up money double the amount he or she has won so far in order to try to win a jackpot.

case: to inspect or examine a house or property with the intent of robbing or swindling.

con: short for "confidence game"; refers to the swindler's technique of gaining the trust of intended victims to ensure the scam's success.

flattie: a con artist who works at carnivals.

fleece: to strip of money or property by fraud or extortion; to charge excessively for goods or services.

forgery: the crime of falsely making or altering a document, such as a check, with the intent to defraud.

gaff: to fix (as dice or tops) to produce predictable results.

good-faith money: a sum offered as proof that each member of a group won't attempt to take advantage of the others. Many short cons focus on taking a victim's good-faith money.

grifter: a person who obtains money by fraud or deception; hustler; con artist.

impostor: a person who assumes the identity of another or creates an imaginary identity for the purpose of deception or fraud.

in the chair: con artist's term for a victim who has invested so much money in a swindle that he or she fears pulling out and losing what has already been handed over.

jackleg: a con artist posing as a skilled professional, usually a contractor of some type, for the purpose of selling materials and services to unwitting homeowners.

long con: a con or swindle that takes a long time to set up, that frequently requires many participants and props, and that can yield a huge amount of money if successful.

mark: the potential victim of a con or swindle.

razzle: a crooked carnival game in which a victim is persuaded to bet increasingly large sums of money to achieve a set number of points and earn lavish prizes.

sharper: a con artist, particularly one who specializes in cheating at cards.

shill: a swindler who acts as a decoy in a con game, posing as a player or investor to convince the intended victim that the scam is legitimate.

short con: a scam that involves a minimum of time and effort on the swindler's part and usually yields a small amount of money.

swindle: to take money or property from another by fraud or deceit.

A Compendium of
Cons and Swindles

begging scam:

A street hustle in which a person pretending to be poor or handicapped collects money from sympathetic passersby.

catalog con:

A one-person short con in which the con artist visits homes pretending to be a representative of a well-known national company. As such, he or she can get the homeowner a discount on any item in the company's catalog. The discount will be equal to the percentage of the item's listed cost that the homeowner pays on the spot. *See also* 10-and-10 deal.

change-machine swindle:

The swindlers place a legitimate-looking change machine near a shopping center's vending machines. The change machine neither makes change nor returns bills, and after a day, the swindlers retrieve it and the money shoppers have lost.

change snafu:

A scam perpetrated on a cashier in which the con artist makes a small purchase with a large bill and then begins asking for change in smaller denominations, until the cashier loses track of how much change he or she has handed out.

fortune teller's handkerchief switch:

After gaining a customer's confidence, a fortune teller informs him or her that a recent run of bad luck can be changed only by getting rid of a substantial sum of money. The customer produces a stack of bills, which the fortune teller wraps in a handkerchief whose ends are then sewn together. The two then proceed to a cemetery and bury the handkerchief, or to a large body of water and throw it in. Unbeknownst to the customer, the fortune teller has substituted the money-filled handkerchief with a paper-filled one en route. In a variation on this con, the fortune teller has the customer flush the money, one bill at a time, down the toilet. (A trap has been installed in the plumbing so that the money can be recovered later.)

front-end swindle:

Posing as a loan officer or a businessman with ties to a foreign bank, the swindler encourages businessmen who need loans but can't get them from legitimate banks to apply to the bank he represents, which in reality is just another swindler with official stationery and an overseas phone and fax number. After pretending to carefully evaluate the businessman's finances, the swindler declares that there is an excellent possibility that a loan would be approved. However, the businessman must pay a loan application fee, which generally is several thousand dollars. After a period of time has elapsed, the swindler regretfully informs the businessman that his loan has been rejected. The swindler, of course, has pocketed the application fee.

gold brick con:

The victim is asked to keep a bar of gold until its sale can be arranged. To show that he or she won't make off with it, the victim is asked to put up good-faith money. The con artist disappears with the money, and the gold bar turns out to be cheap plated metal.

green-goods con:

A gullible if unscrupulous victim pays a small percentage of the supposed face value for stacks of counterfeit bills that the con artist insists are indistinguishable from the real thing. Often, the samples the con artist shows *are* the real thing, but after the victim has inspected the merchandise, the stacks of bills are switched with stacks of cut paper with a bill on the top and bottom.

inspector con:

A con artist posing as an inspector convinces a homeowner that an unnecessary repair is needed, then recommends a contractor (actually another con artist) to do the work. In reality little, if any, work will be done.

money-making machine:

A swindle that, despite its improbability, has been worked successfully on bankers and stockbrokers. The swindler claims to have a machine that not only duplicates currency exactly, but also changes the serial number of the original with a scrambling device. The result, the swindler says, is a perfect counterfeit. The only problem is that the machine takes hours to copy one bill. If the mark is interested, the swindler demonstrates the device, inserting a genuine bill into one compartment and a tray of plain white paper into another. To prove that he's on the level, the swindler remains with the mark the entire time the bill is being copied. The swindler then removes the original and opens the paper tray. On top is a crisp new bill. (The bill was in a false top above the paper tray and dropped down when the tray was inserted.) The swindler encourages the mark to test the "counterfeit" bill at a bank. Of course, it is accepted without question. After the mark buys the machine, it "produces" one or two more bills, which the swindler has loaded into the false top. But after that, the mark will get nothing but plain white paper, and by that time the swindler has had hours to slip away.

Murphy game:

This con has several variations. In the older version, a con artist posing as a pimp solicits customers for a prostitute who is supposed to be in a certain room in a nearby hotel or apartment building. He says that, to protect the customer and the prostitute in the event of a police raid, he will collect the money before the services are rendered. That way, the police will have no evidence that money has changed hands in return for sex. When the customer knocks on the door of the room number he was given, he finds no prostitute waiting for him; by the time he reaches the street, the con artist is gone. In another, less lascivious version, two con men convince several marks that they can get electronics equipment really cheap because they know someone who supervises a warehouse and can steal stereos, TVs, and computers without anyone finding out. All they have to do is show up at a certain time, give their warehouse contact the money, load up the equipment, and drive away. The con artists, with marks in tow, go to a warehouse in a rented van. After collecting the money, they tell the marks to wait in the van until they've talked to their contact and the coast is clear to load up the equipment. The con men enter the warehouse and leave by another door. By the time the marks realize they've been duped, the con artists are long gone.

pedigreed dog swindle:

A con artist enters a bar with a dog and convinces the bartender to watch it for a few minutes while he goes to a business appointment. After the con artist leaves, a second con artist enters the bar, raves about what a fine purebred specimen the dog is, and asks the bartender whether he would consider selling it. The bartender says that it isn't his dog. The second con artist asks the bartender to find out if the owner would sell it for a large sum, usually about $500, and says that he'll check back later. Then he leaves. After a while, the first con artist returns, moaning that his business deal has gone sour and that he's virtually broke. The bartender will frequently offer to buy the dog for much less than the second con artist offered.

Reluctantly, the first con artist agrees. When the second con artist never returns to the bar, the bartender realizes that the dog he has bought isn't a purebred but a mutt.

peekaboo con:

In this scam a con artist puts a valuable-looking diamond ring on the street and then pretends to spot it at the same time as a pedestrian. The con artist says that to be fair, each should get half of the ring's value and then persuades the pedestrian to buy out his share. Often the price the con artist requests is less than half of what the ring, if genuine, would be worth, so the pedestrian thinks he or she is making out extremely well. The stone, of course, isn't a real diamond and the ring isn't real gold. *See also* pigeon drop.

pigeon drop:

A street scam in which a con artist pretends to spot a wallet or pocketbook he has dropped on the street at the same time as a passerby. A second con artist shows up and insists that everyone should put up a sum of money as collateral before they split what they've found. After the found money has been counted, one of the con artists appears to wrap up the mark's collateral money and a third of the found money in a handkerchief and hand it to the mark. In reality, though, the mark's handkerchief contains cut-up newspaper. In another version, a con artist pretending to be new to the big city and frightened that he'll lose his money convinces a mark to bundle up his money with the mark's and asks the mark to hold it while he runs an errand. Using sleight of hand, the con artist switches the bundle of money with a bundle of cut-up newspaper. *See also* peekaboo con.

Ponzi scheme:

In this investment swindle, early investors in a phony business are paid off at great profit with money from a wave of later investors, who, seeing the handsome returns the early investors have garnered, are encouraged to make larger investments. Because the Ponzi scheme requires an ever-increasing number of investors to keep going, there always comes a point at which the money coming in is insufficient to pay off the previous wave of investors, and they all lose their money.

put and take:

A two-person bar con. The first con artist strikes up a conversation with a bartender and shows him a special top that can be used for a betting game. Each side of the top is marked with a *p* (for "put," or pay) or a *t* (for "take," or collect). This top, the con man reveals, is rigged so that if spun in one direction *p* will always come up, and if spun in the other *t* will always come up. The bartender buys the top with the intent of using it to fleece tipsy patrons. Several weeks later, the second con artist shows up at the bar and substitutes an identical-looking top for the original when the bartender tries to fleece him. This top behaves in exactly the opposite manner from the first, and the befuddled bartender usually loses a nice sum of money to the con man.

shell game:

A street con, similar to three-card monte, in which the operator appears to place a pellet under one of three small shells and shifts the shells rapidly across the table. The player bets on which shell the pellet is under. In reality the con artist has it between his or her fingers and uses sleight of hand to place it under one of the two shells the player has not picked as he or she turns that shell over.

Spanish (or Mexican) prisoner:

A time-tested swindle that first appeared in the United States about 150 years ago. The victim receives a letter allegedly smuggled out of a foreign prison (generally it's in Mexico, Cuba, or Turkey). The writer, a prisoner who has been unjustly accused, will rot away in prison unless someone advances him a few thousand dollars (to be sent to a friend at a post office box) with which to bribe his captors. That kind soul will be rewarded many times over, as the prisoner has a large stash of money in the United States where only he can get at it. Thousands of these letters are sent out at a time, and the response rate is surprisingly high.

10-and-10 deal:

Going door-to-door, a con man posing as a sales representative of a national company offers 10 percent off the price of a catalog item if the victim pays 10 percent of the asking price on the spot. *See also* catalog con.

three-card monte:

A gambling game in which the con artist dealer shows three cards faceup, turns them over, moves them around rapidly, and invites players to bet on whether they can pick out a specific card. Sleight of hand is used to ensure that the card the player bets on is not the right one.

Another Side of Cons and Swindles

Mention con artists or swindlers and the image most people see is of a smooth-talking deceiver with no scruples about stealing money from anyone and no regard for what is right or what is legal. But deception isn't the exclusive province of lawbreakers. Sometimes law enforcement borrows the grifter's techniques to catch criminals. When undercover police officers pose as drug buyers or prostitutes, for example, they are in essence working a short con whose marks are street criminals. As with any successful con, creating an illusion is vital, so the police must convincingly look and act the part. But unlike the cons perpetrated by professional grifters—which rely on awakening in the mark through whatever means necessary an overwhelming desire for something—undercover police operations are restricted by laws against entrapment. Simply put, the police may not entice someone into committing an illegal act he or she would otherwise not be predisposed to commit.

This regulation plays more of a role in law enforcement "sting" operations that target high-level and white-collar criminals. Such operations, which resemble the long cons of professional swindlers, may be directed at organized crime, car-theft rings, drug smugglers, illegal arms dealers, or counterfeiters, to name but a few targets. Sting operations typically take months to unfold, which gives targets ample time to investigate and find inconsistencies in the stories of undercover officers. For this reason, sustaining the illusion can be difficult.

Occasionally law enforcement uses the services of a real con artist to give a sting operation an insider's expertise. Such was the case when the Federal Bureau of Investigation hired Melvin Weinberg, an experienced swindler, for the sting that would play out between 1977 and 1980 and come to be known as Abscam.

Weinberg had made a fortune in a front-end swindle—pocketing application fees for loans from shell banks—before pleading guilty to wire fraud, mail fraud, and conspiracy. To avoid a prison term, he agreed to cooperate with the FBI in a probe of white-collar crime.

Weinberg dreamed up the bait: a fabulously wealthy (but fictitious) Arab, Kambir Abdul Rahman (called simply Abdul), whose corporation, Abdul Enterprises, Ltd., had hundreds of millions of dollars to invest—legitimately or otherwise. Weinberg posed as an unscrupulous officer in Abdul's company, which had offices on Long Island, New York.

Initially the sting concentrated on art theft, counterfeiting, and securities fraud. Marks were led to believe variously that Abdul needed forged certificates of deposit from offshore banks to get his money out of his oil-rich Middle Eastern nation, that he was an art collector who had no objection to buying stolen paintings, or that he was looking for all sorts of overseas investments because it was only a matter of time before "Palestinian revolutionaries" overthrew the government of his country and seized the assets of its ruling class.

Two early difficulties that Weinberg and the FBI faced were the operation's small budget, which made convincing marks of Abdul's wealth a challenge, and Abscam's ongoing nature, which meant that troublesome marks couldn't be gotten rid of through arrests because that would scare off other marks. Weinberg's gift for improvising—a successful swindler's stock-in-trade—largely took care of the first problem. For example, when an early mark noted the sparse furnishings at Abdul Enterprises' offices, Weinberg blustered that he was going to sue the furniture company, which had failed to deliver as promised. At a lunch meeting with an FBI agent who was playing Abdul, another mark was served cold cuts instead of the lavish meal that he might have expected. Weinberg remarked that Abdul loved New York deli food and of course could only get it on his rare visits to the United States. And when the mark observed how peculiar Abdul's behavior seemed to be (the agent playing him had no knowledge of Arab customs), Weinberg told him in confidence that Abdul tended to drink a bit too much outside his own country, whose strict Muslim laws prohibited the consumption of alcohol.

Abscam's second big problem—troublesome marks—was handled with a classic swindler's technique called the stall. Many of the early marks had provided counterfeit certificates of deposit and were owed millions of dollars. As the months rolled by and no payment came, they began to grow impatient and to question whether they were being bilked. Weinberg came up with various excuses—for example, he claimed that a large part of Abdul's assets were frozen in Iranian banks as a result of the U.S.-Iran hostage crisis—but he always gave the marks reason to hope that they'd soon get their money. Although it seems hard to believe that counterfeiters, swindlers, and others who have operated on the wrong side of the law could be stalled for too long, one of the things that makes any long con work is that the mark desperately wants to believe that he or she is going to make a big score. Some Abscam marks were strung along for two years.

Gradually, the focus of Abscam began to change as the investigation turned up hints of political corruption. Abdul was said to be interested in building a casino in Atlantic City, New Jersey, and the mayor of Camden claimed that, for a price, he could guarantee that a state gaming license would be granted.

The mayor led investigators to other government officials who could be bribed into doing Abdul's bidding.

As the scope of the investigation expanded into political corruption, another story was concocted: Abdul and his wealthy Arab partner wanted to be certain they would get permanent residency status in the United States in the event of unrest in their own country. This could be ensured if members of Congress were willing to introduce and support special legislation. Before the Abscam investigation closed down in early 1980, one U.S. senator and seven U.S. congressmen had accepted bribes of up to $50,000 in return for promises to support such legislation. In addition, several Philadelphia City Council members and a passel of lawyers had been ensnared.

Masterminded by a veteran swindler, Abscam had ferreted out an astounding range of white-collar crime and political corruption using the same techniques swindlers use to break the law. It had also proved, once again, the con artist's maxim, "You can't con an honest man."

Index

Picture Credits

Every effort has been made to contact the copyright owners of photographs and illustrations used in this book. In the event that the holder of a copyright has not heard from us, he or she should contact Chelsea House Publishers.

page

JOSH WILKER, a writer living in Brooklyn, is the author of numerous books for Chelsea House. He is currently working on a book about revenge and retribution.

AUSTIN SARAT is William Nelson Cromwell Professor of Jurisprudence & Political Science at Amherst College, where he also chairs the Department of Law, Jurisprudence and Social Thought. Professor Sarat is the author or editor of 22 books and numerous scholarly articles. Among his books are *Law's Violence, Sitting in Judgment: Sentencing the White Collar Criminal,* and *Justice and Injustice in Law and Legal Theory.* He has received many academic awards and held several prestigious fellowships. In addition, he is a nationally recognized teacher and educator whose teaching has been featured in the *New York Times,* on the *Today* show, and on National Public Radio's *Fresh Air.*

South Campus
White Bear Lake Area High School
3551 McKnight Road
White Bear Lake, MN 55110

DEMCO